U.S. ARMY

JEN BESEL

BLACK RABBIT BOOKS

Bolt Jr. is published by Black Rabbit Books
P.O. Box 227, Mankato, Minnesota, 56002
www.blackrabbitbooks.com

Michael Sellner, designer and photo researcher

Names: Besel, Jennifer M., author.
Title: U.S. Army / by Jen Besel.
Other titles: United States Army
Description: Mankato, Minnesota : Black Rabbit Books, [2023] | Series: Bolt Jr. mighty military | Includes bibliographical references and index. |
Audience: Ages 6-8 | Audience: Grades K-1 |
Summary: "Engage young readers with information about the U.S. Army. From the group's weapons and vehicles to the people who use them, readers will learn all about how the U.S. Army protects the United States"– Provided by publisher.
Identifiers: LCCN 2021022215 (print) | LCCN 2021022216 (ebook) | ISBN 9781623107611 (hardcover) | ISBN 9781644665886 (paperback) | ISBN 9781623107673 (ebook)
Subjects: LCSH: United States. Army–Juvenile literature.
Classification: LCC UA25 .B45 2023 (print) | LCC UA25 (ebook) | DDC 355.00973–dc23
LC record available at https://lccn.loc.gov/2021022215
LC ebook record available at https://lccn.loc.gov/2021022216

Image Credits
Alamy: 615 Collection, 11; David Wa, 23; Militarist, 20–21; US Army Photo, 8–9; Shutterstock: Dzmitry Kim, 2, 24; Getmilitaryphotos, 1, 5; Militarist, 6; Notto Yeez, 13; Robert Adrian Hillman, 14–15; Route55, 4; vadimmmus, 17; VanderWolf Images, 12–13; Ved Sharma99, 10; U.S. Army: John B. Snyder, Cover; Unknown, 18; YouTube: AMERICAN PATRIOT NEWS, 6–7; 123RF fotoro bs, 18

Contents

CHAPTER 1

What Is the U.S. Army?

U.S. Army soldiers sneak around a building. They **fire** at the enemy. Then they keep moving. They will stop enemies from taking over the city.

fire: to shoot from a weapon

On the Ground

The Army is a part of the U.S. military. Soldiers have many jobs. They fight wars. They build roads. Others are doctors. They work to keep the United States safe.

M4 carbine rifle
fires about 800 rounds per minute

COMPARING ARMY WEAPONS

MK19 grenade machine gun fires about 350 rounds per minute

PARTS OF A

Soldier's Gear

SIMMONS
weapons
gloves

CHAPTER 2

Training

New soldiers have a lot to learn. They start with **basic training**. They build up their muscles. They also learn to use weapons.

basic training: the first few weeks of learning for someone who has joined the military

FACT

Basic training lasts about 10 weeks.

On the Job

After basic training, soldiers pick their jobs. Some learn to **parachute**. Others become spies. Some train to use rockets.

parachute: to jump from an aircraft using a parachute

Where U.S. Army Soldiers Work

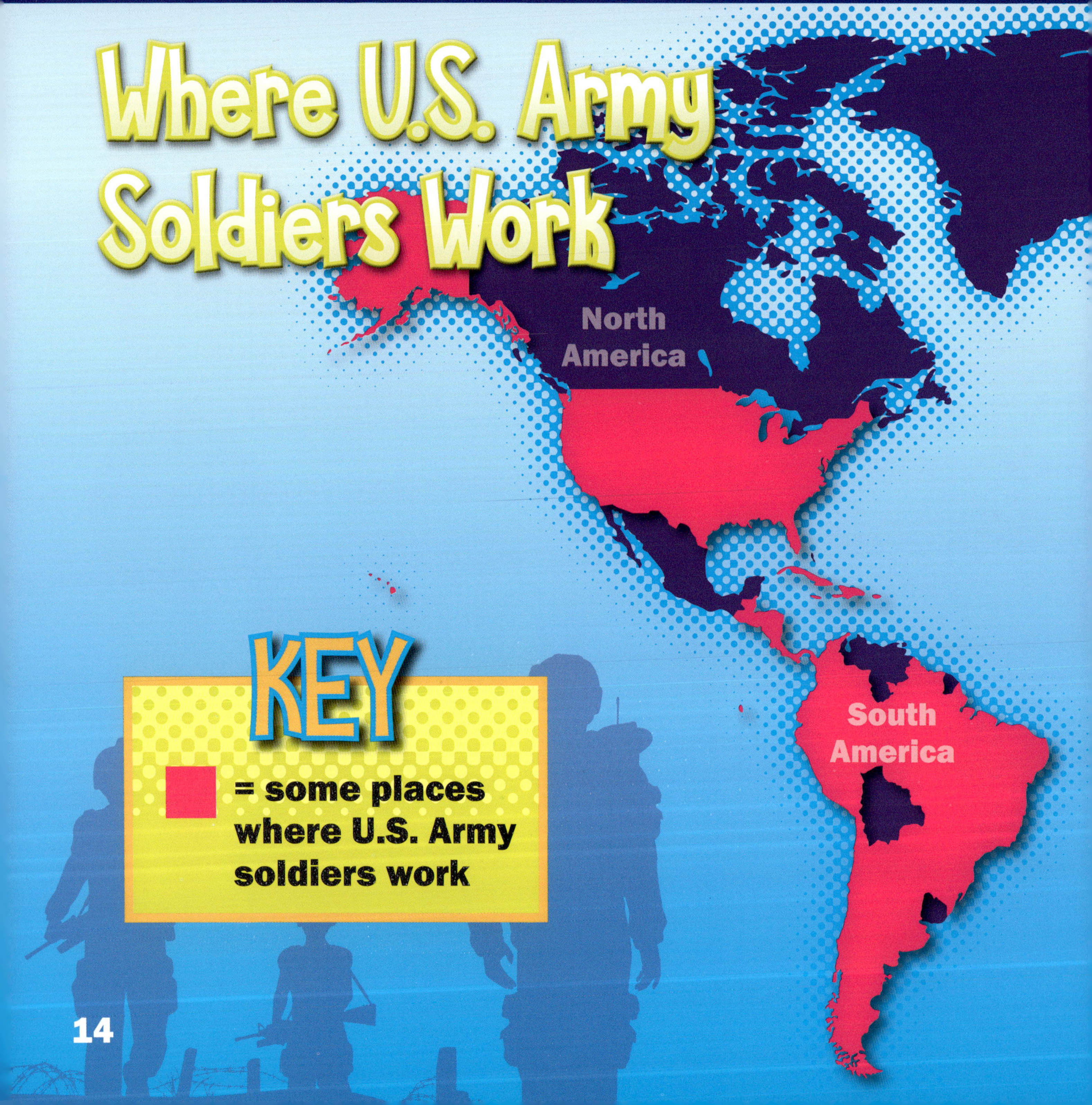

Asia
Europe
Africa
Australia

CHAPTER 3

Gear and Weapons

Every soldier uses an M4 rifle. They use bigger guns for other jobs. They also use cannons to stop enemies.

FACT
The Army uses robots for some jobs.

Tanks

The Army uses tanks to get into dangerous places. The tanks can drive in any weather. They are hard to stop. They keep soldiers safe.

Top Speed of M1 Abrams Tank

about 42 miles (67.6 kilometers) per hour

Bonus Facts

Basic training is sometimes called boot camp.

It is the largest part of the military.

The Army uses dogs to find bombs.

The Army has more than 470,000 **active duty** members.

active duty: a full-time member of the military

READ MORE/WEBSITES

Billings, Tanner. *The U.S. Army.* Inside the U.S. Military. New York: Rosen Publishing, 2022.

Hustad, Douglas. *U.S. Army Equipment and Vehicles.* U.S. Military Equipment and Vehicles. Minneapolis: Abdo Publishing, a division of ABDO, 2021.

Leed, Percy. *The U.S. Army in Action.* U.S. Military Branches. Minneapolis: Lerner Publications, 2023.

About the Army
www.goarmy.com/about.html

The U.S. Army—YouTube Channel
www.youtube.com/usarmy

GLOSSARY

active duty (AK-tiv DOO-tee)—a full-time member of the military

basic training (BAY-sik TRAYN-ing)—the first few weeks of learning for someone who has joined the military

fire (FIHR)—to shoot from a weapon

parachute (PAHR-uh-shoot)—to jump from an aircraft using a parachute

INDEX